# Gateway
## to
## More
## of
## Him

*A Book of Inspirational Poems*

Timothy Wright

ISBN 978-1-64258-150-8 (paperback)
ISBN 978-1-64258-151-5 (digital)

Christian Faith Publishing, Inc.
832 Park Avenue
Meadville, PA 16335
www.christianfaithpublishing.com

Printed in the United States of America

# My Introduction
## Walk with Me

As a ten-year-old, this was my prayer:
"Knock on my window, Lord, if you're really up there."
It was a silly little prayer I would always repeat.
The next thing I knew, I was fast asleep.
But one night when I prayed that prayer,
Three knocks on my window… Was God really there?
Years went by… not a sound from him.
When I gave my life to Jesus, then I heard him once again.
Now some say that he doesn't talk outright,
But I know I heard his voice that night.
Some say, "It's probably in your head,"
But those words he spoke… it couldn't have been.
No… I heard the voice of God one night, asking me to walk with him.
Many years have come and gone since then.
I've longed to hear him once again.
Many trials and tests I've been through,
But those words he spoke… now I know he knew.
He didn't waste one word, you see,
Because every word was meant for me.
And one more word I heard him say;
"Walk with me, please…" he said that day.
I heard the voice of God one day asking me to walk with him.
Many years have come and gone since then.
I've longed to hear him once again.
But those words keep ringing in my ear…
"Walk with me, please." That's all I hear.

# Contents

# More of Him

Did you ever just want more of him? We play the songs; we read the books… We even sing the hymns.

But do we long and do we yearn till our hearts just must return for more of him?

He could catch us up to heaven, and with our lips, we would sing his praise.

Or he could bring us into his presence, and we would praise him all our days.

But sometimes I hear him saying, "If you want more of me, I need more of you.

You must let go of dreams… your dreaming, and every thought I need them too."

So if our hearts are feeling empty and our souls are not at rest, when we're longing for his presence, maybe this is just a test.

To see if in our busy lives we will let him in… so he can open heaven's gates and give us more of him.

# Peaceful Waters Flow

Bring us to that quiet spot as we go about our day;
The place where we can meet with you and our cares all go away.
Holy Spirit, take control… I know you want what's best;
When our hearts are set on you alone, our minds will be at rest.
Past the cares of our day… further we must go;
Beyond the noises in our minds where peaceful waters flow.
A place our heart longs for… a place we can trust.
You have a table all prepared, and everything's for us.
It's filled with all we need today, but we must be moving on.
We'll take it with us as we go and be back before it's gone.
The world's a very busy place… we need somewhere to go.
A place where someone knows our needs and peaceful waters flow.
Why do we get so caught up and hurry through our day?
With so much stuff that's on our minds, we need to get away.
Just give to him your anxious thoughts… He sorts them one by one.
And leave with him your open heart… He'll close it when he's done.
Who cares for us like he does? No one that I know.
So isn't it time you got away where peaceful waters flow?

# A Letter to the Chosen

When God closes a door, you need to walk on by.

That door is probably not for you… Trust God; he knows why.

But if he opens up a door, no man could ever close.

It might not be the door you pick… Trust him because he knows.

When doors slam shut in life, it can sometimes set us free.

Because on our knees we discover hidden manna we did not see.

If we choose our own path, he lets us have our way.

But when life gets hard, we cry to him. "Where is your grace today?"

His grace is where it's always been… His love is ever true.

He'll bring you back… You can start again, but he'll have to carry you.

Life is full of choices… Be careful how you choose.

Because the joy of the Lord is our strength… that we can't afford to lose.

The longer that we walk with him, the more we'll choose his way.

His rod and staff will lead us… like sheep. We tend to stray.

Looking back, who's been more faithful? Who's been our closest friend?

From the first day that he chose us until the very end.

It was him who counted the cost, you see, with a love that was so true.

When he looked down and said, "That one there… I'm going to die for you."

# God Was in This Storm

I'm out in the water, Lord, but I can't swim or float.
If it wasn't you who called me out, I'm getting back into that boat.
This water, Lord, is over my head. Was that you calling me?
I've gone too far to turn back now... The boat I cannot see.
Others who were in the boat, they said I wouldn't dare.
But I stepped out, "Where are you, Lord? I really need you here.
This water's deep, and my faith is small... Lord, what will I do?
I could try to swim to shore, but I would rather trust in you.
I know I have your seed of faith you put inside of me.
But if it doesn't grow right now, I'll be carried out to sea.
How small or big this storm really is, I surely do not know.
But if I didn't get out of that boat, my faith would never grow.
I would like to tell you my faith stood strong until I passed this test.
But the storm raged on... Where are you Lord? When will my soul
    find rest?
Now at last the storm has passed... The sun is breaking through.
Lord, I thought I was all alone, but the storm was really you.
God tries our hearts in the storms of life, so put your trust in him.
Get out of the boat; let faith arise... He'll teach you how to swim.

# Sweeter Than the Lilies

Who are we that you should hear our cry?
Jehovah Jireh, our Provider, the never-changing El Shaddai.
You put the stars in their place and spoke the world into being.
But take the time to hear our prayer. Who are we that you should
    care?
You know our sorrows and our pains and understand all our needs.
You are a shelter we can turn to… You are the God who really sees.
Your name gives hope that we can trust in… It gives strength to face
    the day.
Your name's a fortress we can go to and know our help is on the way.
To you we find our refuge… Abba Father, take our hand.
We're here today and gone tomorrow like a candle in the wind.
But you are strong and you are mighty, and with your strength, we
    overcome.
When life's trials overwhelm us, once again, to you, we run.
There is a name above all others… Go to him if you are bound.
And call upon the name of Jesus?… There is no sweeter name around.
Are you sure you really know him? He is more than just a name.
He's the sweetest Rose of Sharon… The smell of lilies in the spring.
But he will hide among the lilies… only a few will hear his call.
When you find him, you will know it… He is the sweetest rose of all.

# Secure in Christ

Has he not chosen you; you didn't choose him.
And did he not count the cost when he paid off all your sins.
So why are you surprised when he looks inside of you?
And shows you things that are in your heart; things you never knew.
God is living in you. That's always been his plan.
It's what he meant when he said to you, "You must be born again."
There's something deeper going on; it's like a marriage that seals the bond.
He's gone too far to turn back now. He's made the seal; he's vowed the vow.
Nothing can separate him from you... not a demon from hell or things you do.
The cross sealed our bond. You need to understand.
The cords that were tied were tied by his own hand.
He's not a man that he could lie... His cords are strong; his bond is tied.
He lost us once, but never again. The cross has brought us back to him.
Could he love you more? I see no way. He poured his love on you that day.
With thicker cords of mercy and grace, his blood poured out, our sins erased.
So if you wonder how secure you really are...let me tell you once again.
No power from heaven or of hell below could take you from his hand.

# Lord, We Need You

Lord, bring us to that place your disciples must have been.

When you told them you were leaving, their whole world came crashing in.

I know they didn't understand that they themselves would be your hand.

But you drew their hearts so close to you, that loving you was all they knew.

This type of love I think we lack; to put our hands to the plow and not look back.

They knew without you would bring such pain; they would rather be tortured than deny your name.

So move in our hearts like you did back then; draw us closer to you than we've ever been.

Being lukewarm may it never do; give us hearts that will follow hard after you.

Help us Lord to run this race… because you are the prize so you set the pace.

Give us hands that will serve you and a mind that will love you and a heart that will never put anything above you.

This is the prayer that we offer to you… I know by your grace all these things we can do.

# Sharing Our Faith

Lord, how do I share my faith with others?
I've told them you're the bridge over troubled waters.
I've asked them if they were to die, where would they be today?
I've even told them you alone are the only way.
They don't really hang around too long, so I wonder, Lord, am I doing it wrong?
Are people just too busy to spend time with you?
If they knew what they were missing, it would be all they'd want to do.
When they seek you, they will find you because you're never far away.
If they could only see your glory, then I know they'd want to stay.
Now, I'm running out of things to do; is there a better way to tell them about you?
And I'm running out of things to say...there's got to be a different way.
I could write a poem. Yes, that's what I'll do... but I can do nothing Lord without you.
I can put it on paper and pray they'll read if you'll open their eyes and give them faith to believe.

# Last Great Harvest

Take my life… change my heart… make my motives pure.
Touch me in my hidden parts so you can draw me near.
Take my hands and my mind… I have nothing more to give.
If you can break my stubborn will; for you I want to live.
I know the harvest is great, but the laborers are few.
I want to work in your harvest Lord… there must be something I
can do.
When you go to work for Jesus, don't worry about your pay.
You can count your blessings one by one as you go throughout your
day.
He is Lord of the harvest, and when we keep our eyes on him,
Everywhere our feet will go, he will break the power of sin.
Satan has no choice… He must bow to your command.
When it's harvest time and the fields are ripe, we're going in to take
his land.
So whatever you bind on earth, it will be bound in heaven.
And whatever you lose on earth, to you it will be given.
It's harvest time. Make up your mind just get onboard, my friend.
A quick work will the Lord God do to bring his harvest in.

# I Need You

Lord, I need you even now before I start my day.

To fill my heart and fill my mind with only you, I pray.

A prayer like this I realize the world won't understand, but all my hopes and all my dreams I know are in your hands.

And as I go throughout my day, I'll need you even more, to sort and go through things I do so I can spend more time with you.

When the world keeps trying to choke you out,

When it fills my head with fear and doubt,

That's when I'm going to need you more. Only you can make my spirit soar.

It's a wonder how you hide yourself from those who don't know you.

Your glory fills all the earth; it fills the heavens too.

It fills the seas and fills the land; every breath we have comes from him.

But yet you make the blind to see; with eyes of faith they, too, believe.

So the blind can see, and the deaf have heard, what an awesome, amazing

God we serve!

# Do Our Tears Have a Purpose?

We know in Heaven there's not one tear.
So God must have a purpose for our tears down here.
We know that he sees them and he feels them too.
Could they be a sign of what he wants us to do?
If we go forth weeping, bearing precious seeds,
We'll come again, rejoicing bringing in our sheaves.
Do our tears have power to make things come alive?
Can they open deaf ears and give sight to the blind?
Maybe our tears, for all we know, can open blind eyes or save a soul.
When I cry out to the Lord for the blind to see,
That tells me my tears are not just for me.
Lord, help us to labor and work for you.
Until there's nothing left, here you want us to do.
The tears that you give us, may they reach your throne, till the last
   tear we cry and you take us home.

# Enter the Promised Land

Are you searching for him like you used to before,
When you cried out for God and asked him for more?
Or are you walking around in a weary land? The joy you once had you could have again.
Our God is big… Don't think this is it.
The more that you seek him, the bigger he gets.
The more that you love him, the deeper you'll go. The more that you trust him, the stronger you'll grow!
You need to go back and, just like before, cry out to God and ask him for more.
Will you settle for a life that leaves you empty inside?
If you seek him, you'll find him… Our God does not hide.
If your life goes in circles with every new turn and takes you right back, there's a lesson to learn.
This time around, let's try something new… Listen and do what he's called you to do.
By faith, we will enter his promised land or we keep going around and around again.
If the faith that you have you never see grow, then how do you know it can save your soul?
Come closer, my friend, and listen again… The next time around, you need to go in.

# Purpose in Suffering

Lord, you left in such a hurry... I know the battle you fought was won.

But now, I really need to tell you, you left a lot of things undone.

I see a lot of suffering, broken homes, and people too.

What were you thinking? I often wonder. So now I give my thoughts to you.

"To the world suffering has no meaning, but to my own, it will be clear.

Because when you suffer, you will notice that's when I always draw you near.

And when you suffer for the kingdom, you do my work till I return.

And all the work I left unfinished, I left for you so you can learn."

The hardest things you ever suffered, you see the Father understood.

And all the years you thought were wasted he was using for your good.

There's not one thing that goes unused... God's weaving all things in his plan.

Not for one moment did he forsake you because all things are in his hand.

So when you suffer, there's a reason. That's how he proved his love for you.

You'll only suffer for a season. Now don't forget, he suffered too.

# Precious Moments

Precious moments are when we're trusting you, and the path is hard to find.

But when we look back, it was plain to see you were with us all the time.

Or when we're still and alone with you and your glory fills our hearts,

And you heal our scars when we let you in as you search our deepest parts.

The mystery of your love keeps us longing to see more,

When now and then you show us something we've never seen before.

So show us more and tell us more, and hear us when we pray.

You are the one whom we adore… We need you more each day.

When life gets hard and trials come, be there to calm our fears.

We know we can count on you… always faithful through the years.

Precious times are when we give you praise, and the words come alive.

When you touch us deep down in our hearts, tears will fill our eyes.

Those tears aren't there because we're scared or because we don't love you;

They're only there because we remember all the things you brought us through.

# Don't Forget Who You Are

When you're faced with an enemy that's bigger than you,
Some say that surrendering is all you can do.
Or if the mountain before you looks too big to climb,
The same people will tell you you're wasting your time.
Unless you know the one who put the mountain there,
You'll walk away defeated... all those voices you will hear.
Have you forgotten who you are? Let me tell you once again.
You're a child of the King... sons and daughters of him.
This mountain before you is not too big
When the one who made it inside you lives.
Defeat is not an option with God's sword in your hand.
Your enemy will bow down at the voice of your command.
A victory cry went out when Jesus died on that cross.
"It is finished" is still sounding... Satan knows the battle's lost.
Even death has been defeated... There's no temptation you can't bear.
You see the stone's been rolled away, and his body isn't there.

# The Watchman

Lord, if I ever doubt your love for me, remind me of how I used to be.

Take me back to when we first began, and show me the person I was back then.

Year by year, as I grow in your grace, I sometimes forget the pains you erased.

Don't let me complain about things I go through but look at the way you're making me new.

Would you put a watchman before my mind to remind me life's trials are your design.

Don't let me pretend that I love you so; search my heart, oh Lord… I want to know.

So I can worship you with a heart that is right and truly say you are my delight.

Start a fire down in my soul. Lord, hold me close… don't let me go.

I want my life to count for you. Help me to finish what you've called me to do.

I know the cross will be my friend. This life I'm living one day will end.

Then all I could be will be gone for evermore. Lord, help me today before I reach that shore.

# A Glimpse of You

How can I write about how great you are when you are so much greater than everything by far?

I couldn't even tell the story without a glimpse of all your glory.

If I could paint, I could never paint you… All the colors in the world would never do.

You are far greater than what we know or see, but I could tell the story of how much you loved me.

You took me out of darkness and brought me into light.

I was a mess from head to toe… I must have been a sight!

But you loved me with a love I have never felt before, and when I showed you all my sins, you loved me even more.

Who am I that you should bother or even really care? My past forgiven… my sins erased… just like they were not there.

And if that wasn't enough, you gave me hope I'll be with you. It is the anchor of my soul when trials I go through.

So how could I not tell of the love and kindness you give to me? My life was empty… I was bound in sin before you set me free.

I love to tell my story because you gave me a brand-new start… You can't find it in a book because it's written on my heart.

# God's Word Is Faithful

What if God's word is really true? What if those who are saved are only a few? Are we living for Jesus, or are we too busy livin'? Do you think that heaven is just a given? To work out our salvation… What does that mean?

And why did he say, "With fear and trembling?" Straight is the path, and narrow is the way. You sure don't hear that preached much today.

So can we trust that none of God's word is wrong? Or can we pick and choose? Now the struggle goes on. I've been down that road. It's filled with despair. I finally decided there's a reason it's there. What would we overcome if we could pick and choose? I'll do this one and that one, but this one I refuse. No, it makes more sense when we leave God's word alone. Otherwise we would be tempted to put us back on the throne.

Now here's where we struggle, and it's important that we do, because the word of God will come alive. That's why he said "a few." So rejoice in all your struggles because narrow is the way. Fight the fight; run the race… The word of God will set the pace. He will be faithful to his word… faithful to the end… and all God's people said, "Amen!"

# The Doorway to My Heart

I know the struggles in your life… I can feel your pain.
Don't forget my love for you… Come near to me again.
I am not a fairy tale or a wish upon a star.
But everything you need in life… I am near to you, not far.
I formed you in your mother's womb and watched you struggle in
   the night.
I long for you to trust in me and make me your delight!
There's a doorway to my heart… a key that you must find.
It unlocks your heart to me and makes you only mine.
Take my hand and follow me… I will guide the way.
Through life's storms hold tight to me, and I will be your stay.
The peace that I have for you is greater than your fears.
There are no boundaries to my love… always endless through the
   years.
Look for me in everything as you go throughout your day.
Without me you are not complete… I made you just that way.
When I designed your heart, there's something you should know,
I left for me the biggest part… that's so my love can grow.
The cross will open a door for you and unlock your love for me.
It is the doorway to my heart… just try the key and see.

# Filled to Overflowing

Do you know God knows all your thoughts? Believe it or not, it's
    true.
All your dreams, all your fears, and everything you do.
You can tell God all your secret things you would never share.
He puts them in the sea of forgetfulness, and he says, "No fishing
    here."
You say there's sins you won't give up… sins you like to do.
With God you really don't give up… You trade for something new.
When I gave to him my pennies, he is very generous you see.
I reached inside my pockets… Gold coins were given me.
He satisfied the hungry heart with more than it could hold,
And filled it up way past the top until it overflowed.
So bring to him your deepest hurts, and see what he will do.
And also sins you struggle with… He even takes them too.
Bring your questions, bring your doubts, bring him everything.
I challenge you to bring them all till there's nothing more to bring.
Beyond your dreams, beyond your hopes, beyond what you've been
    told.
There is a love God pours in us… our hearts could never hold.

# A Martyr's Call

Lord, we can't do this without you...... It's our desire to give our all.

But if we had to, would we do it? And could we die a martyr's call?

Many brave have gone before us... "Make us strong like them," we pray.

The songs we sing... they are the chorus... still speak and move our hearts today.

Holy Spirit, it's you we turn to... our precious treasure from above.

Without your help, we would deny him... Take away our selfish love.

If you take away our comfort, give us faith as pure as gold.

And when the flames of life get hotter, make us stronger; make us bold.

Till the day we stand before you, keep our hearts, oh Lord, we pray.

To all the martyrs that went before us, you are the heroes of our day.

One glimpse of you... it will be worth it. Pain and suffering will be no more.

The seed you planted will finally open beyond the grave at heaven's shore.

So may we never, Lord, deny you... With our last breath, we'll see your face.

It's not how we start that matters... It's how we end that wins the race.

# Lord, Go Deeper

Are your motives pure? Is your heart true? Because God, who is all-knowing, can see right through.

This is the place where I'm tested the most. Because deep in my heart are my motives exposed.

When you hear yourself saying, "Lord, it's not fair," let God go deeper to see what's down there.

Sometimes the things that irritate you might be just a sign of what God's trying to do.

So instead of resisting and say it's not fair, let God go deeper to see what's down there.

Search us, O Lord, and help us to see no matter how painful or hard it will be.

You alone can help us to heal when you take out the hurt and the pain that we feel.

We'll sing your praises when you are through, because the freer we are when we're trusting in you.

The next time you're hurt or filled with despair, you might hear God saying, "I'm working down here."

With every rejection you've felt, every hurt you've gone through...

Remember he was rejected and hurt just like you.

# Passing the Test

Can your faith stand the test? How's it do when life's a mess?

Or what about if you're all alone. No one's watching, no one's home.

Because faith that's not tried is no faith at all. It's okay to stumble, but it's not good to fall.

So are you angry with your brother? God gives a warning here.

You could be in danger of hell's fire… This flame is hot… Do not get near.

So how are you doing on this little test? Should we keep on going, or do you need a rest?

God's word reveals sin, but it's like a two-edged sword.

Now I have to deal with mine, and you have to deal with yours.

You see, it cuts both ways. It reveals my heart too.

So don't think these words were meant just for you.

Did we mention forgiveness? That's a hard one to do.

God can't forgive us when we don't forgive too.

This test is over. That's it; we're done. But remember with God, his test goes on.

# God's Rest

As I go throughout my day, I see empty faces along the way. Then I stop to understand... There is no peace without him.

I see them laughing when they're on their phones, but do you ever watch them when they're all alone?

I go to prison, and they tell me there... When the lights go out is when people fear. So at night, when you go to bed, do you have peace with Jesus, or is there fear instead?

Because perfect love will cast out fear... Have you ever asked Jesus to help you here? Fear has torment that's not from above. Stay close to Jesus; there's power in his love.

Just remember you're in a real war... That's what all your armor's for. This war is of a different kind. You'll need God's helmet for your mind.

When you trust Jesus as your Lord, the word of God becomes your sword.

Your eyes will be opened, and then you'll know... that Satan is your real foe.

Your enemy hides in dark places; that's why you fear. You'll need to just get out of there. Satan's spirits are weary, and they're searching for rest. If you hang out in dark places, you're a perfect nest.

To come out from among them, you'll need your shield. Satan has no power when to faith you yield. You'll also have freedom of a different kind; God's word living in you will control your mind.

The peace that you feel, you won't understand. But when the lights go out, you'll sleep again.

# Have You Been There?

I searched for a quiet place where my soul could find rest. But your still waters run deep… Even this is a test.

Lord, how can I go when your way I can't see? When the waters get deep, all my fears will find me.

"I won't lead you in life where I will not go. When you pass through these waters you will see that is so."

In quietness and confidence, I will make my way. I can hold to this anchor… It will be my stay.

I have been through the fire… It was years ago. You stood by me then… Now those flames are but coal.

Faith will arise, and these waters will still. I will trust in his leading… I will trust in his will.

The battle kept raging till I took a stand. Though the water was deep, my faith could see land.

This was a battle that brought me much gain. I discovered the power I had in his name.

The fears that I had… they would finally reside. When I went through those waters, something happened inside.

The faith he imparted would conquer my fears. It was worth all my struggles… It was worth all my tears.

No one could buy this… even riches untold. This was more precious… More precious than gold.

# His Majesty

There is none like you, O Lord… No, there is none that compares
to thee.

Who but you makes mountains tremble and at your rebuke can calm
the seas?

Search the heavens, and you'll discover there's only one upon the
throne.

Beside him, there could be no other… He is God and God alone.

He sent redemption unto his people and revealed his grace forever
more.

He has a name above all others… It's King of kings and Lord of lords.

All creation tells his glory… Oh, that we would do the same.

Praise him… Praise him… He is worthy. Lord of lords and King of
kings.

We know the heavens cannot contain him, but where his glory fills
the throne,

Those who trusted him to save them, this is the place they'll call their
home.

Oh, worship him all you his people for he has power over the grave.

No other name is found in heaven… whereby we can now be saved

Those who love him will see his glory when he sits upon the throne.

All creation will bow before him for he is God and God alone.

Praise him now for all he does and all he says he's going to do.

We worship him who reigns forever surrendering our hearts to you.

# Only One Way

Is God really mean? That's what people say. You'll all burn in hell if you don't do it his way.

Wait a minute here... Let's think this thing through. Is God really mean? Is he really that cruel?

If you're on a sinking ship and you hear the captain say, "Everyone to a lifeboat... It's our only way."

Would you think that he was mean or that he doesn't even care? No, you would get into the lifeboat... It would be your only prayer.

This world's a sinking ship... going deeper into sin. Jesus is our lifeboat. Are you on board with him?

At the click of a mouse, you can go places you don't want to be. Going deeper and deeper into sin... there's no bottom to that sea.

There's only one way up... I can tell you what to do. Get into the lifeboat... It can rescue you.

When Jesus was in the garden, he cried out, "Is there another way?" Heaven was silent... not a word did the Father say.

He went from the garden to a rugged cross; there on Calvary he bled and died for sinners just like us.

Because God so loved the world that he gave his only Son, so if you're looking for another way... trust me, you won't find one.

# To You Who Are Hurting

In quietness and confidence, you'll find your strength in me.
When life gets rough, don't forget that I can calm the sea.
When the storms of life are all around and it's getting hard to stand,
I can be your anchor. Because I can calm the wind.
I sometimes allow your enemies to cause you a little pain
Because I know when I deliver you, you'll cling to me again.
I saw you on that day when you surrendered your life to me.
Not one moment have I left your side… every hair on your head I
    see.
So when your world around you goes upside down again,
Trust in me with all your heart. Reach out… You'll find my hand.
For I have chosen you… You have not chosen me.
You are the apple of my eye. All your struggles I do see.
You might not understand every trial that comes your way,
But remember this: I am the Potter, and you, my child, the clay.
One day soon you will look back, and it will be plain to see,
With every trial that you went through, you're looking more like me.

# Do You Have the Right Jesus?

Do you have the real Jesus? I pray to God you do.
Because there's a lot of them around, but only one is really true.
Does he have your heart, and are you trusting in him?
Is he Lord of your life, or is he just a good friend?
The real Jesus has a cross he gives to me and you.
And on that cross, he showed the world what real love would do.
The heavens were watching on that day as darkness filled the air.
You know it wasn't just the nails that held him up there.
Our debt was so great; it took his blood to pay the cost.
Did you know that it was love that held him to the cross?
So do you have the right Jesus… the one who died to set you free?
The one all heaven's eyes were watching when they nailed him to
    that tree.
He could have called ten thousand angels to take him from that cross,
But don't you know if he did that, we would still be lost.
So if you have the right Jesus, there's a cross you bear today.
And that cross to you is precious because it took your sins away.
So don't be fooled by another Jesus… there's only one in all the land.
You will know him when you find him… He has a nail print in his
    hand.

# What Is Love?

Are you growing with Jesus every day? Are you learning to trust him along life's way?

Did you know faith, hope, and love remain, but if you don't have love, your faith is in vain.

Now this is love… It is patient and kind. It can't be bought… It can't be sold. You learn it in hard times.

It's easy to love those who love you; that's like loving ice cream and chocolate too. Real love can endure much pain, and when life gets hard, real love remains.

So don't think love is easy to do, it's the greatest of all, but it will really cost you. Love can suffer and endure much pain. Real love is tested again and again.

You might have big faith and with your hope you stand tall, but if you miss love, you miss the greatest of all.

Love is tried in the fire… God will test you, my friend. The flames will get hotter when God's burning off sin.

Your love will grow stronger with every test you go through when you yield to the one who's working in you.

The problem today is people don't understand love. If you're learning from Hollywood, that's not love from above.

Love will hardly notice when others treat you wrong. It is quick to say, "I'm sorry… We need to just move on."

Love is the greatest because it's the hardest one to do. Jesus went to the cross and said, "I love you."

# God, Change Us

Don't be surprised when you go through your day,
If God sends you people that rub you the wrong way.
I find every job all the places I go.
Those people are there; somehow they just know.
Did God really send them to try to change me?
Could it be in my heart these people I need?
This is one thing that he tells us to do…
Pray for those people who persecute you.
His hand might be on them if they went astray.
He'll deal with their hearts, but he tells us to pray.
People around us are tools in God's hand.
Sometimes he calls us to suffer for him.
I don't know why suffering is part of God's plan.
I do know in heaven we won't suffer again.
Just remember, my friend, you are heaven bound.
Be faithful to Jesus… He'll give you a crown.

# A Real Friend

Everyone wants a real friend that will always be there.

They'd know your thoughts and know your dreams and always seem
to care.

And when things in life would bring you down, they could cheer you
up just being around.

When life gets hard and you get burned out, they're always there to
help you out.

Isn't this the friend our hearts long for? The kind of friend you want
to see at your front door.

But the truth is with people, they can let us down. And sometimes
the ones that hurt us the most can be the ones that were so close.

Now there is a friend that is closer than a brother. You have the same
father, but you don't have the same mother.

He is a friend who knows just what you need. His name is Jesus…
He's a friend indeed.

I found something in him I never found before. Then I realized he
was the friend I was looking for.

There were times I turned my back on him, and I know I hurt him
so.

But he did something different then… He would not let me go.

Then I knew he was the kind of friend that would love me always to
the end.

# God So Loved the World

So what are you going to do with Jesus? Is he just a legend from times of old? Did you know he said he was God... Now that was pretty bold.

He was either the biggest liar the world has ever seen, or was he God like he said he was? This often troubled me.

Did he know what he was saying? Had he gone off the deep end? He said that he was God. I Am... the Great I Am.

That's why they crucified him... They hung him on a tree. But death couldn't keep him in the ground because he was God, you see.

Sin had entered into the world, and it passed from man to man. So all creation was under sin till the cross when God stepped in.

It was love that kept him on the cross; His love for you and me. Till the power of sin was broken, and he paid your penalty.

Because God changes everything; that's what his love can do. We are broken people in a broken world, but he can make us new.

Jesus had to come into the world to break the power of sin. Time stood still, erased itself, and started over again.

We went from BC to AD.... Did you ever think about that? Over two thousand years ago, God did something new.

He erased everything and started again... He can do the same for you.

# In Your Presence

He who created the heavens in just one day could have written a
   poem that would take our breath away.
He might have written about his Father or a place called Beulah land.
Or maybe of his kingdom or his coming back again.
But he saved those poems for you and for me so we could tell about
   His love throughout all eternity.
So I'm storming heaven's gates with God's word as my course.
He said the violent, you see, will take it by force.
I want that poem… My soul can't rest. Right from his heart… noth-
   ing more… nothing less.
Oh, the wonder of his glory we could never take it in. But if a poem
   could tell the story, I would write it with my pen.
He could show us streets of gold, pearly gates, or crystal seas. But if
   we looked into his eyes, we would say, "Lord, none of these."
Let us stay here in your presence… It's you we want to see. You are
   all our souls have longed for, and where you are, we want to be.

# Sowing Seeds

You say you got excited once, you even shed a tear;

The word of God touched your heart… That's really nice to hear.

Jesus talked about a farmer who sowed seeds along the way.

Some fell on rocks, others fell in thorns, the birds took some away.

But some also fell on good ground… What's Jesus trying to say?

The word of God is like a seed… To make it grow, there's things you need.

A listening ear and believing heart can give this seed a perfect start.

So why all the fuss with this little seed? In God's great wisdom, he had a plan; that with the foolishness of preaching, he would save man.

To those who won't seek him with all their heart, the seed of faith won't even start.

So if the cares of this world is where your heart is found, your seed probably landed on stony ground.

Or if God's word really means nothing to you, it's probably choked out with all the things that you do.

So let me help you if I can to see what went wrong; take a good look within.

# It's About Time

So where are your thoughts as you go through your day? Is your mind set on Jesus? Did you take time to pray?

The time to decide is when you get out of bed. Will you rush through your day or seek God instead?

It's the little foxes you know that destroy the vine, and it's what we don't do with the thing called time.

Everyone has it… no more or no less. Just twenty-four hours… did you know it's a test?

Tomatoes get ripe when they stay on the vine, but there's one thing they need… they need lots of time.

It's not the warm nights or the bright sunny days; it takes time for a tomato to reach its last stage.

If we're quiet before him, his seed starts to grow. When you're faithful in life, your fruit starts to show.

I was not faithful as I went through my day, not thinking of him or stopping to pray.

I spent years of my life going nowhere with him; I had to go back and start over again.

When I did go back to give him my all, the seed that he planted was still very small.

But he stayed right there when I went away, he was watching and waiting for me every day.

He is the Good Shepherd…ever true to the end. He waits for his sheep till they all come in.

# Taking out the Trash

Do you only go to God when there's nowhere else to go? Is he like last on your list of people that need to know?

Or maybe you just dump on him… unload all your trash. You give him all your rotten stuff… the things you know won't last.

Now people like that can really get you down, so you need to just excuse yourself when these people come around.

God knows all of our troubles that we bring to him each day. But what really makes him happy is when we praise him anyway.

He is very patient, and his compassion has no end. So if you want to make his day, begin to worship him.

No matter how you're feeling or what you're going through, if you praise him in everything, he'll want to be with you.

So praise him in the morning before you start your day; before you're up and running… take some time to stop and pray.

If you walk with him, he'll walk with you… If you talk with him, he'll talk with you too.

A grateful heart is what God needs… It's like honey to the bees. So if you've been complaining that God just can't be found, maybe you need to keep a little honey around.

The next time you complain about what people put you through… maybe you should ask yourself, "Have I been dumping on God too?"

# Free Indeed

Jesus heals from inside out… Do you need his touch today?

We're not born broken people… We just get broken along the way.

Because we all have broken dreams, and broken dreams make broken hearts.

Did you know your Maker sees the crack before it even starts?

Only he's the Great Physician … Only he was without sin.

Only he knows where to touch you and make you whole again.

If life has left you broken and also left you pain, I have good news you need to hear… There's help in Jesus's name!

The first step is the hardest… Just walk; don't try to run.

But when you feel him take your hand, your healing has begun.

By now your outside's doing good, but your inside needs more time.

Because he heals from inside out. When he's done, you'll do just fine.

Now if you were to do nothing to try and stop this pain, his power inside you dwindles, and your life begins to drain.

All the dreams that could have been… one by one they too will end.

There will be bumps along the way… but his grace is all you'll need.

If you continue, you'll hear him say, "Whom the Son sets free is free indeed!"

# To You Who Will Listen

To you who are hurting now, give me your ears, and I'll tell you a story passed down through the years.

The story's unending… the message still true. Pay attention, my friend… This could be for you.

This is a story the proud will not hear, but you who are hurting, come now and draw near.

Pain is God's phone… Is he calling today? Are you going through life but not looking his way?

So for you who are hurting, this could be God's test. He says, "Come to me, and I'll give you rest."

This story is repeated down through the years… When we cry out to God, he really hears.

But those who are proud will go their own way. "That's for the weak, not for me," they will say.

It is for the weak, but with God, we're made strong. I'd rather be weak and be right and not wrong.

To you who will love him, this message is clear… We find that through suffering, our hearts are drawn near.

To you who are proud this does not apply, but neither will grace on the day that you die.

# It Will Be Worth It!

Promotion doesn't come from the east or the west. Promotion comes from the Lord.

Are you trusting in him, or are you trusting your flesh? You see, his word can cut like a sword.

It reveals our motives… We cannot hide like a light shining into the dark.

So watch what you say before an all-knowing God who can see through your words to your heart.

God has a season that he will exalt us, but first, he must deal with our pride.

Don't cover it up but offer it up… There's nothing before God we can hide.

So search us, oh Lord… We surrender to you. Your grace is sufficient, we know.

Because when you're finished and when you are through, our garments will be whiter than snow.

Although it is painful, this work must be done. God's preparing for himself a bride.

Without spot or wrinkle and washed in his blood, we are sealed with his treasure inside.

So lift up your hands you who are weak and praise him for all he will do.

This work that he started he will complete… He's the one who is faithful and true.

Just remember one day you will be with him… the one that our hearts do adore.

Every tear that we cried he will wipe from our eyes and our trials remember no more.

# News Flash

Now I'm not a preacher, but I have something to say.
I don't want your money, so put your wallet away.
Consider your ways… before God only will you stand.
Are you stashing your cash and giving pennies to him?
Now when you give, do you give from your heart?
Or do you give what's left over… the smallest part?
Now here's a news flash… This might be for you.
God won't bless your money if that's all you do.
So if things just keep breaking, and you can't get ahead,
And it feels like you're living right on the edge,
This sounds like something God would do
To get your attention so he can bless you.
When the Father corrects us, he does it with love.
So we don't miss the blessings that come from above.
Now if you're not a Christian, this does not apply.
You may have lots of money, but you won't when you die.

# Are You Searching?

Are you tired of wondering what life's all about? I mean, why are you here? Have you figured it out?

Maybe you're chasing all the dreams from within to find when you have them, you're empty again.

Have you ever considered something new in your life? It's not a new husband, a house, or a wife.

The things of this world are not going to do. You'll find when you have them, sometimes they have you.

Will you spend your whole life to come to the end and take a look back and be empty again?

Are you ready right now to figure this out? To find out what life is really about.

If you're searching for something to satisfy you, then God is the one who you should look to.

He'll fill every need that your heart's longing for, then fill it again... just a little bit more.

Till you're overflowing with his blessings from above, you'll stand back amazed at his incredible love.

You can spend your life searching, but you're searching in vain. You'll never find fulfillment even close to the same.

Don't take my word, but I'll say it again, he'll fill you much fuller than you've ever been.

# Nowhere to Turn

When my faith is tested, I see how frail I really am.
I have nowhere to turn, so once again, I turn to him.
Those bridges that once led me astray,
I burned them all… I'm not going that way.
You are the way; I have no other plan.
God's path is very narrow, but it will lead me straight to him.
I surrender my heart; I give you full control.
Where you lead me, I will follow; where you call me, I will go.
You have taught me from my youth that I can always trust in you.
Proving yourself faithful makes it easy now to do.
Looking back through the years, you have never left my side.
When the path was hard to follow, you have been a faithful guide.
You have always gone before me. I know I can trust in you.
Here's my heart… If I don't give it, I would surely be a fool.

# Faith in Action

Two farmers were trusting God for rain.
One, when he prayed, went and planted his grain.
One didn't plant because deep in his heart,
He wouldn't trust God till he saw the rain start.
So my question to you will be pretty plain.
Are you planting your seeds, or are you waiting for rain?
So why aren't you planting to a world lost in sin?
When the Father sends rain, your seeds won't be in.
Are you worried about people and what they will say?
Or are you saving your seeds for a rainy day?

# Indescribable God

You can't put God in a picture frame; he's not at all like this.

He's way too big for your fireplace, and there's a lot you're going to miss.

He's a God of love and a God of war and a God of peace and so much more.

He holds yesterday, today, and forever in his hands. With our little minds, we could never understand.

His attributes are innumerable; his ways past finding out.

He's the Lord of lords and King of kings; if you've ever had a doubt.

He always was and always will be eternal and forever God Almighty.

The alpha and omega, the beginning and the end, the creator and Sustainer, all things come from him.

I hope you're getting the picture… He's really big, you see.

He holds the universe in his hands; he's not like you and me.

The earth is just his footstool, and the heavens are his throne.

But what makes him even bigger yet, our hearts he calls his home.

And out of all of his creation, the cross cannot compare.

He redeems lost sinners like you and me, and he does it all right there.

You see, when he created the heavens and laid out all its plans,

He forgot just one thing … He forgot all of your sins.

That's when mercy left a trail for all of us to see… It started at the heart of God and stopped at Calvary.

Have you found that trail? It continues to this day. It's going to take you to the cross and wash your sins away.

# Are You Winning the Battle?

So what's your purpose in life… your goals and your dreams?
Is God in your thoughts, or is your mind filled with things?
Is your to-do list so long that for God there's no time?
Are the toys on your shelf all stuck in your mind?
Examine your heart… Is that something you do?
So the things that you have don't really have you.
Our hearts are a gift from God above
Because before all things, he wants our love.
Are you willing right now to examine your heart
And to take out the things that keep you apart?
If you listen close, you can hear God say,
"Leave room in your heart for me today."
There's a battle going on, and you're in it to.
It's not over money or land, it's for you.
Our commander is Jesus… He knows the way;
He's been here before… He can help you today.
Our hearts are the treasure that we're fighting for
Because who has your heart will win this war.
If you're trusting Jesus, this battle you'll win.
Don't trust in your heart… it will deceive you, my friend.
"If it feels good, just do it" will lead you astray;
And the cross you once cherished will get in your way.
Sin's fun for a season… we all will agree,
But the cross will bring joy for all eternity.

# Guard Your Heart

This message is for someone… Maybe it's for you, if you go online
for pornography like lots of people do. Einstein said, "Cigarettes,
they have no power over me. I've quit over a hundred times… it's
as easy as can be." Addictions are hard to break… This is God's
plan.

Because when we struggle to come out, we think twice to go back
in. That's why they're called addictions, but the truth can set you
free. You can't replace real love with what you're watching on TV.

Did you know that when you lust, you walk through Satan's door?

With an appetite that can't be filled, you'll just keep wanting more.

But if you go through God's door, he can set you free.

Just in case you didn't know, he created sex, you see.

It was never meant to be perverted… It's a gift from God above.

But if you misuse it, you will lose it and get lust instead of love.

If that sounds like you, this could be the reason why…

You're replacing love for a picture and believing Satan's lie.

It's very sad to see the damage of what pornography can do,

It can destroy real love forever… I hope that isn't you.

# We Will Pray for You

Can I tell you a little story? There was a prince from Galilee.
He didn't hang out in high places; not where a king would usual be.
He spent his time among the people… No bodyguard, no FBI.
He felt their pain and knew their sorrows; the people came to find
   out why.
The hearts he touched left all to follow. They gave up everything.
He made them feel he really loved them even though he was a king.
We won't forget about your sorrow. We will surely pray for you.
But there's a king who sees your sorrow; there's so much more that
   he can do.
You will find him where people are hurting…that's where he always
   seems to be.
He will even bear your sorrows, and if you're bound, he'll set you free.
So cast all your cares upon him because he really cares for you.
And you will find when you are grieving, he is grieving with you too.

# Saying Goodbye

When I'm gone, his face I'll see,
So if you cry, don't cry for me.
Cry for those who've lost their way
Because I'm in my Father's arms today.
Pray for my loved ones whom I hold so dear.
Tell them I'll miss them, but I'll see them up here.
But most of all, most of all, love God with all your heart
So we'll all be together… let not one depart.
I treasure the moments that we had to share.
I'll be there to greet you when you get up here.